12 Months From Now...Book III

(It's actually been more like 24

...but who's counting)

SIR FINIS DeMILO BREWER

12 Months From Now...Book III

12 Months From Now...Book III

Copyrighted 2014

By: SIR FINIS DeMILO BREWER

Published by:
TOOSWEETPUBLISHING productions
PO Box 6512 New Orleans, Louisiana 70174
Website: toosweetpublishing.com
email: toosweetpublishing@yahoo.com

Printed in the United States of America

Library of Congress Cataloging in Publication Data

ISBN: 978-0-941091-18-3

No part of this book may be reproduced or transmitted by any means electronic, mechanical, photocopied, recorded, or stored in a retrieval system, without the written permission of the Publisher.

First Printing

September 12, 2014; 11:45PM
FRIDAY NIGHT

I've just finished the last entry of Book II; unfortunately it didn't end like I expected. The last 10 months of my very "topsy-turvy" life was not included; and the reason for most of the exclusion was due to the craziness of my "topsy-turvey" Life. Quite a few of the incidents caught me off guard, and left me with very little options. We all know that the lack of money can restrict a lot of what you can, and cannot do. My lack of a job, not having a bank account was definitely putting a damper on my activities. Once my original Lab-top started acting like my ex-wives (tripping), I had no choice but to bring my writing to a screeching halt. I still wrote long hand whenever I was inspired, but my handwriting is so bad, that even I sometimes have a hard time reading it.

I've had the pleasure of keeping my Youtube, Twitter, and Face Book accounts active; posting a new video whenever I got the chance, and sending a few "tweets" as the latest "news" hit the wire. I even got a few "tweets" when I comment on the death of Robin Williams; his passing was such a shock. And even more so when we learned that he took his own Life.

My circumstances are far worse than his could ever have been, so I just don't see it. Oh how I wished I had just 5 minutes with him. I know I could have help change his mind about leaving...so soon.

If you got a minute, check out my "social

web pages"; for Face Book I have two accts. The first is my personal page: "SirDemilo" is how you can get to it. The 2nd account is my Ministry pages; if you are not a Minister, or you're not involved in ministry, then don't bother dropping by. I only post ministry information on this site. It is found under the infamous name of

"Jammin4Jesusproductions".

And of course my favorite site is my You Tube channel: "SirFinis", And then there's my Twitter page: Sir Demilo or SirFinis as well.

I've posted some pretty informative stuff, so check it out.

Well, I'm getting tired, I need to find a spot and hit the sack. Mosquitoes & some tiny disgusting little bugs that I can't seem to catch or see is tearing my legs up. It's not as humid tonight as it has been, so I guess I can find some long pants to put on. These "suckers" are so bad that I was tempted to called fire down from heaven to burn these "buggers" to a crisp. But I guess that would be over-kill (excuse the pun); I guess I can just get a can of Raid for those "sap-suckers"...that should end their short little lives a bit sooner.

...Goodnight; I'm gone.

Chapter 2.....Wednesday, Sept. 17, 2014

Well, it's been a very good day; from 7:30 in the morning to about 12:30 noon, I wrestled with trying to email the final draft of another manuscript I've been working on. The "ending" and final page was typed almost a week ago. And since its been completed, all I needed to do was proofread, and email to Printer. Well, I'm still having difficulty.

The software "Office2013" has decided to provoke me to "cuss" and "make my day"... but since I don't used foul language except for "dam", muckin jerk", "ass"(rarely), and "Ahhhhhhh!", I decided to just take a deep breath and find some Computer help. "All Points Computers" on GenDeGaulle was a lifesaver. Trampus the owner, in 5 secs re-booted "microsoft WORD" and got my files to open. Twelve hours later, the computer was still trying to uninstall the trial version of "Office" that I installed 7 days ago. I started my documents with this software, but have not been able to finish, so it has delayed my getting the manuscript:

"The GHOST in the Fourth Bedroom"

to the Printer by 4 days, now going on 5. After this mess, I spent the rest of the evening with my older brother Larry. He wanted me to show him where our lil Sister Mildred lived; he haven't been to her house cause he didn't know how to get there, so I gladly made the trip.

It being Wednesday, I was gonna try and make it to City Church later on for 6:30 pm (I only recently just started going back to church), but I rode with my brother in his car so staying for service was out of the question. My truck "bluee" was still on the westbank, and with my current situation, I didn't have the luxury of going to "the East" (as it's called by us natives) but once a week. And barely then due to gas prices, an 8 cylinder engine, and Texas license plate problems. What's the plate problem? Long story... let's just say I have to pray before, during, and after every time I get in my car to go anywhere. And we know it's been said that GOD watch over "babies & fools"; well I think he has add a category called "broke, unemployed Christians," because nothing but the grace of GOD has gotten me to church, and everywhere else, without any problems from the police...or "po po" (ghetto slang). So I saved my weekly trip to church for Sunday to make it to the 11o'clock service, and /or 9'oclock service, if I'm up early.

Last week I didn't have any money, and with no gas in my car I knew I wasn't going to make it to church by the time Sunday roll around. But GOD fixed it so that after helping a stranger (now fellow friend-Artist) move some items from out of her storage unit where I hang-out, she blessed me with $20.

"Now Artlette, you know I didn't do this for money."

"I know, but you really helped me out a lot, and GOD wants me to give you something."

"Well, thanks."

And then the next day I helped my cousin with a electrical problem over at her rental property...another $20 bucks. As much as I has helped her now, and in the past it should have been more like $2000 dollars, but she don't have any more money. And when she did have some, (thousands & thousands of dollars from what she has told me), I was either not living here in New Orleans at the time, or my services wasn't as valuable. Because when folks have money, they get quotes and pay professionals. When they are broke, they call friends like me.

I've been a participant in this "abusive friendship cycle" most of my life, but I fault no one but myself. I had a hard time saying "no" to people; especially if I knew I could get the job done. But a few years ago I had to learned how to say "NO," and to say so without any guilt. Even though the Bible says,

"When it is in your power to do good, do it."

I've learned that the key to this scripture is knowing when something is good, and when something is not. And if a friend or relative only calls you after all the money is gone and they've paid all the professionals, then that's...

"Not good".

I had to in my own nice way, teach them how to continue to call all the professionals, because "Sir's Handyman Service" was no longer open for outside jobs...if SIR didn't own it, SIR no longer worked on it.

After receiving the $20 from my cousin, I knew then that I would make it to church, pay my $4 tithes, a $2 offering towards the "Gideon project" and about $8 left for the rest of the week.

"Jack" the guest from Gideon told an awesome testimony; when he finished I had tears in my eyes and felt the message for the day had all ready been given...

"...For GOD has made provisions for our lives even before we were born;"

What an awesome testimony!

Since seeing Jack, I've already added

"Gideon" to my list of organizations to bless..."when the time comes."

I've been able to make it to church three Sundays in a row now, and I'm very thankful to GOD for the privilege...and it is a privilege. I still haven't gotten a job though; one of the hospitals called me, but I never heard from anyone again even after making a personal appearance. When I spoke with the two different departments in person (ER & ICU) it sounded as if they were for certain going to call me with a schedule. September 8, 2012 was the official day that Baylor Hospital unjustly fired me; and then unjustly refused my unemployment. But its all "good in the 'hood" as some say; $84 a week puts gas in my car, pay my phone & storage, feeds me, and gets me the essentials. From $4500 a month two years ago, to $334 a month is a big difference, but as "Paul" once said...

"Life gives you lemons; smile, make the drink, and enjoy the ride".

Don't sweat the lil stuff; GOD is still in control; got our back;...and HE will have the last say.

Each Sunday, City Church gets more & more interesting; I saw something this Sunday when the Bishop was contributing his portion to the service, but I won't comment yet. I'm going to allow the Holy Spirit to continue to give me understanding concerning the matter. City Church is unique, and very different from most traditional church environments. I hope all the members could just see what I see, and realize the depth of what GOD is saying through this ministry. But I'm sure not all do.

"Like Life, church does not have to be boring; and most importantly like Life, you can "Love GOD, keep HIS commandments, and still have fun."

And that's just one of the insights I see with City Church; it's a little example of worship & praising GOD and learning about the "deep things of GOD". But at the moment, right now.. City Church is only scratching the surface of the "deep things of GOD."

MY GETTING BAPTISTED FOR THE 2ND TIME IN MY LIFE...

When I got baptized the Sunday before, I'm sure a few wondered,

"Why was SIR...the "Soul"man getting in that liquid grave...

...I THOUGHT HE WAS A MINISTER!"

What they didn't know was, I was just following orders. Several weeks earlier, I had a very profound dream. And in it I entered a church and someone came up to me and say,

"Come on, you got to get ready for the baptism."

And of course, like in real life I had not made planned on getting baptized again; I was baptized on my 12th birthday.

So when I awaken, I began to wonder what did the dream mean, and I began to question GOD.

"Ok LORD, what are you trying to tell me?... Am I wicked? Do I need deliverance? From some kind of weakness?

(skinny girls with a pretty face, good morals, and shy & quiet)?"

Am I wrong for feeling like Job sometimes (like I've been cheated, robbed, dealt a bad hand)?"

Well,...as pondered the matter, I began to realized that if I got baptized again, to do so now would be the 40th anniversary of my first time being dipped in the watery grave. Then I thought, "40 means completion"; so

I figure maybe it is GOD getting ready to take me to yet another level (who knows)?

So for several weeks I wondered; even wondered about what church should I be baptized in, or even if the church mattered. At the time of the dream, I hadn't been to City Church in at least 6 months; No gas, no money, car broke, needing new rear end, no job, no place to live. In other words, if anything bad could happen during this time in my life,...it did.

Also during this time I got a chance to go to Illinois for a week to video-tape a ministry conference. It was my friends church (Seventh Day Adventist), and I'd been helping him with video shoots for the past two years. I had made the promise months earlier, so I make it a point to try and keep my word. He paid for my travel expense to Texas (megabus); I lend my services as cameraman, director, host, etc., and I keep my vow to him, and to GOD.

While at the conference, a young woman got baptized during this week, and I was even wondering if GOD wanted me to get in the water as well. But after I listened to the vows the young lady was being asked to repeat & vow to keep in honor of the Adventist religion, I knew it was not GOD, and not for me to get in that water. Because GOD knows...I don't do religion! Or, promote religious doctrine other than the "pure religion" of James 1:27..."to visit the fatherless & widows in their affliction, and to keep himself unspotted from the world."

So the Sunday I came to City Church, it had only been my 2nd Sunday being back after being out for almost 6 months. When I left for church, I left home prepared with a change of clothes, just in case GOD wanted this conference at "City Church" to be the one I get baptized the second time around. I was still a bit uncertain when I walked in the sanctuary, but when I thought about the theme of the conference (Elevate), I said,

"WOW!...LORD, you really got a sense of humor".

Then I laughed to myself as I signed the paper, and got myself prepared to enter the "liquid grave" again. Thinking about it at first I thought to myself,

"Maybe there is some old dirt or past sins that I need to wash off."

Whether there was or not, it didn't matter what anyone thought; I knew I didn't have the dream for nothing, and I wasn't taking any chances of disobeying GOD.

When I first started going to City Church more than 14 months ago, I was gung-ho about being involved with the various aspects of the ministry. Then I heard about the 20+ years some of the leaders have put in working side by side with the Pastor, and I feel out of place.

I know GOD called me many years ago, and the first 5 years of my Ministry training at the church where I was installed as Youth Pastor, I brought the message every Youth Sunday. Then after my divorce (from the marriage & the church), I spent another 5+ years as the Cameraman behind the scene at a different church. Yet every Sunday I longed & wanted to be called up to preach and bring the message at this church.

"Oh LORD, is today the Sunday? Are you gonna let Pastor Mike point to me and let me today, bring the message you place in my heart for your people?... Uhhh, Lord?"

This question was posed to GOD almost every other Sunday, if not every Sunday. But it never happen; and looking back, I had as much chance of preaching there as I had of winning the Lottery three consecutive weeks back to back.

After this church, I spent the next 7 years at two or three other churches as a member. By then I wasn't all that interested anymore about being behind the pulpit, or dealing with youths for that matter. Youths I'd learned by then, were a different breed than when I first started out. And I was finding that many didn't care much for church, or GOD for that matter. They were the start of the "Internet Generation," and the most important things to them were: the latest

Rapper, Beyonce, ipods, flip-phones, camera phones, myspace, video games, and texting. And I just didn't care to relate to them anymore. From the ages of 2yrs to 11 yrs, it seemed easy to get children to have an interest in GOD. But it seems that by the time they reach 12 or 13 yrs now a days, they are doing & thinking the same thing that their non- church upbringing peers are doing and thinking. Pregnancy, pre-marital sex, and even lesbianism is now rampant amongst this generation...

"Being "Gay is ok"; and even if you dabble, there won't be a need to squabble. Because whatever you like, is definitely alright!" seems to be the attitude of this young generation.

So by the time I got to the "Potter's House and sat under the leadership of Bishop T.D.

Jakes, I was just another member. With the fire to preach still burning within me, only now the flame was very low.

With having seen & experience so much involving church & my life as it pertains to the ministry GOD gave me, I'm very cautious and hesitant now about being involved in any aspect of church business. Sometimes I feel like the last thing I want to do is be noticed, or in the spot light. So in spite of the years I have in the Ministry, I find myself intentionally keeping a low profile where ever GOD sends me.

I love City Church, and I know after 14 months (including the missing 6 months straight) of being at CITY CHURCH, I'm there for a reason. I'm not sure what, but I know I have been called to play a part in the "ushering in of the 2nd Coming of Christ". But "I ain't saying nuthin..., I ain't doing nuthin"; because I'm very cautious now about making mistakes, people thinking I'm trying to make a name for myself like some do, or trying to be friends/"buds" with the pastor. I have NO room for any "mess" in my Life, and have no desire to bring any, in anyone elses life. Life for me has been crazy enough for the past 20 years; I have no time for drama. And plus, mistakes are no fun; and will only make Life...

... less enjoyable. Been there; done that.

A few minutes ago I was reading a book called "Only Love Is Real" by a psychiatrist named Brian Weiss. It's a very good book, and holds some very interesting insights about Life as we know it. I think it holds some views that will send the church community in an uproar, but it speaks some very interesting truths. And, because I know GOD has taken me down some pretty crazy roads concerning TRUTH, I believe this is also why I'm reluctant about being in the forefront of any Ministry. But in spite of my reluctant, I know if it's a "can of worms" that GOD wants me to open up to the "Body of Christ", HE also know I don't have a problem with ..."thus says the LORD!"

At the moment I'm reading about 14 books I picked up from the library today, on various subjects, working on finishing two manuscripts to get to the printer by the end of the week, and in the process of writing the 3rd book of the "12 months from now" series. Try to Pray at 3am most nights, and be up at 7am; all this while not having a job, no cash at the moment, no place to call MY Home at the moment, no law of the land vehicle, only the WORD of GOD to depend on. And to make matters worse, I don't see or get to talk to my three daughters that were becoming three recognizable faces at City Church, because of their foolish mother's Lies, crooked lawyer, & corrupt court system. But there is no need for me (or you) to worry...

...for the Word of GOD says,

1. " I have never seen the righteous forsaken, or his seed beggin bread...";
2. "Vengeance is mine, I will repay...";
3. "The wealth of the wicked is layed up for the just..."

       ...and,

4. "The "JUST" shall live by faith...".

I AM SIR...the SOULman; and I do not live by bread alone, but by every WORD that proceedeth out of the mouth of GOD.

Chapter 3....Thursday Morning, September 18, 2014

I finished the book that I mentioned earlier; the one by Dr. Brian Weiss called "Only Love Is Real". I won't go into great detail about it, but if you get to read it, it will change your perspective about a lot of things you believe. In the course of my own journey of life, I've been taught some very profound things that have altered my view about a lot of things I once believed. And using the Word of GOD as a reference, I've often found that my new belief was often confirmed in the Word of GOD. For example, the book talks about reincarnation. The closed-minded thinking of the religious community has taught us that this is absurd. And of course I grew up sharing this belief. Now that I've "grown", I think that there is some truth in some of it. But here is where the mistake is made. Like the term psychic, often the wrong name or label is given to a truth. And this is where the problem comes in for the Christian; and this is what causes the immediate rejection of the belief. The term "psychic" & "reincarnation" belongs to the New Age world, or Occult. And we know this to be the "darkside" or evil. But to have the ability to see into the future is a gift from GOD called "Word of Knowledge". All the Prophets had this gift; both old day Prophets & Prophets of our day. When I learned of the Prophet Edgar Casey many years ago, I was blown away by the "gift" that GOD had given him. At the time I was working at a hospital in Flagstaff, Arizona, and an older Nurse who was more religious than "Christian" overheard me mentioned his name.

"Oh he was a psychic, I wouldn't mess with books about him", she said distastefully.

I of course continue to learn about the life of Edgar Casey and was continually blown away by his life. The fact that the "gift" came to him as a child after falling asleep with his head laying on the Bible was proof enough for me about where the "gift" came from. Or proof, of whether he was a Prophet or a New Age Psychic.

The term "past-lives" would be a more appropriate term, than the term "reincarnation". For the Bible says the "Soul" never dies; along with quite a few other things concerning the subject of "Souls". After reading "Only Love Is

Real", it will confirm without a shadow of a doubt "that the Soul never dies", and WE all have been here before.

For years now the Lord has had me dealing with the subject of Homosexuality; I even recently wrote a song (and working on the video) that will blow the lid off the belief system concerning this matter. I was going to save the details for a conference I would love to host one day, but I guess I can introduce the "revelation" here. The conclusions I've come to I've given it the name of "Gender confusion" or "Identity crisis".

I believe that the people that are caught up in this "masquerade of sexual confusion" were more than likely the opposite gender in their "past-life". So the attributes and tendencies of the gender that they were before, has somehow spilled over into their present life. Why this has happen?... I'm really not sure but I will continue to ask the Holy Spirit (maybe they spoke something in their previous life; it is said that there is "Life & death in the power of the tongue).

And if you know your Bible, you also know that it says that in Heaven we will be neither "male" or "female". So in other words, since the "Soul" is the one that exist in Heaven (and not the physical body), than the "Soul" is the one that is neither male or female. But this is where I require further investigating.

And when it comes to people dying and coming back to life, most if not all of the stories about "NDE" (Near Death Experiences), the family members that has previously died, are always recognized by the newly departed person.. And the family member they recognize is always a mother, father, sister, brother; etc. In other words, they are still maintaining their gender as they were known when they were living here on earth. So there has to me more to this gender matter.

When it comes to Homosexuality, I believe it is a demonic spirit falling under the spirit of Confusion. & Deception.. And this spirit works hand-and-hand with the evil spirit of LUST.

It is sexually driven, and fueled by the spirit of perversion.

I have also discovered that Homosexuality is also the result of a muti-generational curse. Where the "Enemy" comes in at is, he infiltrates the persons mind at an early age in their present life making them think they are the opposite sex than their physical bodies shows. Then the infiltration becomes a sexualize force. And this force is called "LUST".

The Bible says we wrestle not with "flesh & blood", but principalities, & spiritual wickedness in high places. So the person is already struggling thinking they are trapped in the wrong physical body, when the TRUTH is...the feeling is just an illusion. The "gender identity" struggle in this life is not REAL. It feels very real, but it is not! Then to make matters worse, the enemy comes along and "sexualize" the struggle. Now the person thinks they are attracted to the same sex, when it comes to sex. But my suggestion is simple, if they would just drop their underwear,

they would get an epiphany:

"Wow! I got a vagina, so it must have been designed by GOD for me to be attracted to persons with a penis...wow!"

All over the world, the "gender confusion" & "identity crisis" would be non-existent if people would open their eyes and look at the "equipment" they are working with. Check out their private parts, and the person with the opposite private parts will be your clue. Everyone would know what sex they should be attracted to, and having SEX with.

"Same sex" goes against the "Laws of Nature", and Creation cannot create or be fruitful, under natural & normal circumstances. Which GOD specifically has commanded, ALL (Man, Plants, & Animals). But satan's whole purpose in life is to defy, and upset the plan GOD, and go against everything GOD says to do. So hence we have the problem that we have in today's society.

I've learned in this Life, if you are closed

minded, and hang on to your old beliefs, leaving no room for the Holy Spirit to teach you, you will NOT grow. With every Life, we are to grow, & learn, create, and worship GOD (no other). I have been taught many things by the Holy Spirit; a wealth of knowledge & information. And in this LIFE I'm living now, each day is a "transformation and a revelation" of new knowledge & information. And GOD placed the Holy Spirit here on earth with us, to guide US into these "TRUTHS"...

...into ALL Truth."

And TRUTH can only come by the Spirit of Almighty GOD. For satan is the "father of Lies".

As I close, a thought popped into my mind last night as I was reading "Only Love Is Real". The thought was about my ex-wife & I, and it blew my mind. I thought,

"Lord, that's Crazy...that's the crazies thing I ever heard of!"

"...We are the "past-life SOULS" of Gomer & Hosea". How crazy is that thought! But that's what came to me as I was reading the book "Only LOVE is REAL"

Then I remembered what the Lord spoke to me about my wife when we first got together. He said,

..."the Book of Hosea".

I didn't know what he meant at the time, but it was as clear as day; and I've never forgotten those words.

Years later, the same words were repeated out of the mouth of one of my best friends after leaving Bible study one night. At the time, the wife was committing adultery, and I was questioning who this "crazy person" was that my wife had now turned into after 6 years of a beautiful relationship, My friend was at Bible study this particular night, and called me after leaving church. When I answered the phone she said,

"That is your wife!...and the LORD said read the Book of Hosea".

Of course she didn't know how profound of a statement she had just made;...but I did. And I never questioned again whether the "divinely appointed" young wife of mine was really my wife. Never again did I question GOD, or her "divine appointment". In spite of what she had done, and was still doing, GOD said,

"Yes, she is YOUR wife".

Now two year later, I'm reading "Only Love Is Real" and I'm given a revelation about my beautiful young wife & I that just blows my mind completely...

...Then I savored it for a moment. Then I say,

"Lord, that is crazy!...absolutely crazy!"

Then I just accepted the crazy thought, and realized it might explain a lot of "crazy" things in my crazy life. What was the crazy thought that came to me?

"I was the Prophet Hosea in my past-life; now I'm SIR the Prophet in these "last days".

"My young beautiful wife...

...Gomer the whore in her past life; and now Usheeka, my young beautiful wife the adultress in this life."

I told you the thought was crazy! Welcome to my world..

It's been crazy since the day I was born; when look back, I just shake my head. Constantly trying to understand it all.

Born at 7 months (2 months premature), the enemy tried to kill me before I got here. But GOD said,

"...not so."

Baptized on my 12th birthday in '73; I always felt there was something to this event happening when it did…and on my actual birthday.

Had a thirst to know GOD, and didn't know why; I was even envy of Moses, Samuel, David, & Elisha…of how they "knew" & walked and talked with GOD, and GOD knew them. I wanted that for me to as a kid.

Growing up, I read the Bible without being told, and wanted to know GOD for myself;

I also didn't believe in fooling around, drinking, or cuzzing, yet, I knew how to still have fun.

At the age of 33 yrs old, I was called to preach; I wanted to walk & talk to GOD like Moses did; and wanted to be like the Prophets of old like Elijah, Samuel, Elisha. Let's just say from the very start, my life was different from most. And as we climax to the final hours of this "earth age", the craziness of my present Life continues, as we prepare for the greatest event since the birth of Christ. The arrival of His 2nd Coming, and the start of the next "earth age", as written in the Holy Scriptures.

Sunday morning; 12:30 am....
September 21, 2014

I know I should be sleeping, but I'm not tired anymore. Just finish watching a movie called "Tomboy"; it's a French foreign film. I tend to prefer foreign film, documentaries, and movies that most would think are boring. I checked "Tomboy" out, and a few others from the library (the two others were called "Dirt" & "Egypt's Lost Cities"); the latter two were kind of boring, but "Tomboy" was good.

In light of the "gay climate" that so many that are "out" are enjoying now, it's a very interesting topic. A girl being a Tomboy when I was growing up, didn't have any gay or homosexual tones or connotations attached to it; but being a feminine boy did. In the black neighborhood you heard,

"Stop acting like a little sissy, ya big a baby"; or,

"Look at that punk over there; look how he's switching when he walk"

And if you were in a white neighborhood you heard,

"Hey there you little faggot!"

So whether you heard faggot, punk, or sissy, every neighborhood had one. But a girl being a "tomboy" back in the day, was no big deal. She hung out with the boys, played football with the boys, and even got a little sexual harassment from the boys from time to time. But it was never crossed our minds that she might one day grow up and have sex with girls...simply unheard of.

The interesting part of the night though, was a surprised phone call I received while watching "Tomboy". It was from an old friend I used to work with at Home Depot years ago. He was "in the closet" at the time, but I always knew of his "struggle" with his gay-ness. .But I went on and let him think his secret was safe with him & GOD alone.

During that time that we worked together, him and his wife was splitting up. And I knew it was probably because of his urge to "climb the fence," was getting too strong to continue living as a heterosexual married man. But this phone call "out of the blue" must have been very liberating for him, because the "cat was now out the bag". Not only was he telling me that he was gay, but he had come out of a very abusive one to booth. And I was a reasonable person to talk to.

Of course he was surprised to know that I already knew of his gay-ness. We talked for at least two hours or more, and I even discuss how the Lord is giving me revelations on the subject. I even informed him that I have several books coming out in a few weeks, and one of them specifically deals with the subject in a very surprising way. As I ended our phone call, I thought about how it is always good to hear from an old friend. And even better when you can talk to that friend about anything, and no subject is off limits. I guess he needed to talk to an old friend that was more understanding than he realized.

Overall, the day has been good. I got a chance to bring an idea to the local library for my children's book promotion. I truly don't believe it was my idea, because the thought just hit me out of the blue. I guess they will get back with me by next week and let me know if the idea has been approved & accepted. If so, I'll be telling "True Ghost Stories" in celebrating and promoting Literacy, along with the atmosphere that the month of October brings. You know...that candy time of the year.

I'm still having difficulty with the software to send the manuscripts to the Printer though, but I'll just pray & leave it in GOD's hands as I wait for the finances to fund all the projects. While walking on the Levee earlier today, I got another idea for a Concert on the River. The set-up would be pretty awesome if I can get to do it. It would be a concert/festival held in JULY (7th month) every year. I would call it the "ThankULORDJESUS" festival; a spectacular Laser/Light show Musical Concert featuring some of the greatest Gospel Artist & other Genres of music that is not ashamed of thanking GOD for HIS goodness, and HIS grace that HE has shown unto us.. Of course it would be produced by "Jammin4JESUS productions".... I can picture the whole event even now! What an awesome "Praise fest!

Well I need to get some sleep; got to get to church in 9 hours & 33 minutes. Not sure if I'll be taking the bus, or my car; not much gas or cash at the moment, but it'll all work out.

My friend Gwen, and her Mom & sisters should have made it back from Vegas earlier today. I haven't talked with her yet, since being called from Vegas to fix some siding at her sister's Vern's house. When she called me she said,

"I forgot all the things you know how to do Finis. Could you hang some siding on my house to satisfy the insurance company's requirement for renewal."

Yes, the Lord has blessed me to be able to do, but people tend to call me when they have No money. They pay the other guys when they have money; and call me when they don't. But I've learned how to say "no" when I need to; I might be very gifted & talented, but "Mamma ain't raise no fool".

While CeCe's "Throne Room" plays in the back ground, I guess I'll lay my butt down and try and get some sleep. I mentioned to my boy Tre earlier while talking to him on the phone, that a few things had changed in my life. I told him I was now divorced again, and had to start all over for the second time. And even though I was sitting in a 10x10 storage unit that's doubling as a bedroom/office, I was fine. I know the LORD has promised so much more for me, and this "box" I'm in is temporary. When I move in my house(s) (I've already picked out), the only thing that will change will be the furniture. I will be content because it doesn't matter to GOD where you live. It's HOW U LIVE, that matters to GOD. So whether you are living in a tent, or bedding down in a mansion, as long as your LOVE for GOD doesn't change because of "things", I'm sure GOD has no problem giving you the "desires of your heart"...even if it's a big 10 bedroom mansion.

...Buenos noches, me hermanos & hermanas; Voy con DIOS!

Tuesday morning...September 23, 2014 12:22am

Well, I been so busy that I didn't realize I made no entry concerning Service on Sunday. I went to the 9am service and stayed for the 11 o'clock service as well...OMG! Pastor was "off the chain" singing at the 11am service; the early group don't know what they missed. Wow!...it was awesome! Talk about being satisfied; I was just talking about that before the service. I'm at a place of contentment that I don't think I've ever been; and I don't think it has anything to do with anything externally. I've lost every house I've own (total of 10); at least 30 cars; opportunities; wives; money; time with children; the list goes on and on, but I'm good! GOD...is still...GOD!

I can't do much writing right now cause I'm high, high, high. When I listen to certain music, that's what it does. I've never needed any drugs or alcohol to make my soul float, or my mind take a trip. Music does it, and always has. That's why I don't and cannot listen to anything. Music speaks to the Soul, and each type of music has a different affect on the soul. Its either positive and helps the soul to grow, or its very negative and destroys the soul, or it creates a destructive force within the soul.

No Artist or musicians took me on a spiritual journey while growing up, like Earth, Wind, & Fire...unbelievable the places I would go spiritually. If you looked in my eyes after a session, you would have thought I'd been smoking something, drinking something, or just trippin on something. Certain gospel music takes me to a different place all together, but all gospel like all music doesn't have the right spirit. So I'm careful about what gospel music I listen to as well. One of my favorite is a CD put out by the DayStar singers; it has a cut on it called Adonai...what a song! I take off in seconds. I can truly say that music affects me on a spiritual level like no other, and it has all ways been that way. I see and feel things that are sometimes too much for words.

After service, I spent the day by my sister like I do almost every Sunday since getting a chance to go back to church. She is just one exit away, so it's only right for me to visit with her for a bit. She is my younger sister, but the oldest out of the 4 that I have. The other three are triplets, and of course they were spoil rotten growing up, by all of us.

I soon left and headed to my little office/abode; after 7pm I wouldn't be able to access the property, and that also means that when I enter before 7pm, I'm locked in for the night. So I usually try to do whatever I need to if I decided to stay on the premise. It's not really allowed, but the manager has been very gracious and just overlooks my staying. He knows my situation, and he always asks how I'm doing. My response is always,

"I'm fine!"

...cause I am. Many would expect me to be disgruntled, but I've forgiven all (including myself) and decided to enjoy this life because that's what we all are here to do. Many things encroaches upon these enjoyments that we are suppose to have like Lies, deception, hatred, greed, immorality, polluted religions & evil religious practices, etc., but if we just LOVE...it fixes ALL the "ills" of the world.

I've been doing a lot of reading (& writing) lately and it's literally changing my Life. I'm getting revelations, and finding out" truths" that could turn the belief systems of society on its head. Truths that once you look at real closely, you can't deny them for being that... TRUTH.

...If you are a seeker of knowledge, especially knowledge of GOD, expect your mind to be blown, and things you once believed, to be discarded or revised. A few close friends & family may think you have lost your mind... In other words, gone crazy, but the Bible says,

"...where the spirit of the Lord is, there is liberty."

Some Christians may read this and still

deny the truth of what it is really saying, but anything that feels like bondage, or involuntary restraints its not the "Spirit of GOD" that is in operation. I've seen this numerous times in the church; the Spirit of the Lord flowing like a breeze, than someone stands up and pushes their idea & opinion on the congregation, and the Spirit just leaves. But because it's how it's been done (tradition/ritual), no one questions the practice & the Spirit of the Lord is quench and there is no room for the LORD to move and do something different. Or, work a miracle in the sanctuary/.

Well I've learned to Look, Listen, and ask GOD, and HE always gives me revelations about some of the simplest things. Little things that some might not think are a big deal; yet the enemy is using to slowly rob the "Body of Christ. Robbed them of knowledge & revelations; gifts & wisdom; miracles & truths; and just simply the presence of Almighty GOD. That was one of the many lessons I learned in my early years of training with the Holy Spirit. People have good intentions, but the road to Hell is paved with a lot of good intentions. I learned that sometimes the same people that are praying and waiting on GOD to move, or the same ones that are holding him up, or has HIS hands tied. Look at the Jews for example; they don't believe that JESUS has already come, and was born in a manger. When I first learned of this I was floored; how can the chosen people of GOD be so clueless and in the dark about Christ? ...It didn't make any sense. But I learned a great deal from this; their practices and traditions is what keeps them ignorant of the truth, and the LORD moving in their lives. In other words, they are waiting on GOD, but GOD can't move because they are their own problem. And in many churches today, that is still a problem. Their traditions & weekly rituals is what's keeping GOD from moving in the sanctuary. Many will verbalize that the "spirit of the Lord" is present, but if it really was, no one would have to talk about it. The tangible evidence of HIS presence would speak for itself.

Well, I got to go; ...I got to pay my water bill & my gas bill. Must have been that old chicken I ate a few hours ago. Until later...GOD Bless!

Sunday,....September 28, 2014   9:00pm

Whew! Just awaken from a nap; the day has been long. I've waited several weeks for this day, and it is finally here...and what a day it has been...

...Jesse rocked the house!

But then, thats what Jesse do; Jesse Duplantis that is. Ain't no "M.O.G." like this Man of GOD. In two months, it will be 20 years since the Lord spoke to me about this "mantle of ministry" HE placed upon me. Jesse Duplantis was one of the first "TV preachers" I was introduced to. And the LORD spoke to me very clearly back then and said,

"You see him...He's an example of the

scripture where it says the "first shall be last, and the last shall be first.

Then the Spirit of the LORD went on to explain to me that Jesse was one of those types that didn't fit the image of a "servant of GOD" or Preacher. But GOD said the traditionalist (religious people) have had their chance. They were the first, but they made GOD a religion. So GOD raised up people like Jesse (and myself) to help make GOD a FATHER again in the eyes of his people. Jesse Duplantis comes from a "rock band" background with drugs, women, & partying. But he had a...

...PRAYING MAMA,

and GOD answered those prayers of that "praying Mama" and little Jesse's life has never been the same. I thank GOD for him in so many ways cause, being called to the Ministry GOD knew I needed someone that

I could relate to. I didn't have time for Liars, Thieves, & Whoremongers (religious church folk) who taught...

..."do as I say, and not as I do".

I heard the stories growing up; I even had members of my "family tree" who were "supposedly" preachers, but they had a compromise lifestyle. They came from out of town every holiday, and the stories that would be over-heard by inquisitive little children would leave their little minds wondering; I was one of those little minds. But as I got older, I put "two & two" together and came up with four. Not three, and not five, but four; and I knew what I saw preachers & "Reverend so & so" do as a little boy, was not ok. I knew I wasn't gonna be, and didn't want to be, like what I heard, or what I had seen growing up. And way back then almost 20 years ago I said,

"Father GOD, I've studied the lives of a few other great Men and Women of GOD like John G. Lake, Smith Wigglesworth, Katherine Kuhlman, Amiee McPherson (to name a few), and I notice something with all of them. They seem to have started off well, but things didn't seem to end so well. But LORD,...

...whatever you are calling me to do, I'm not interested in failing. If I have to fail, find someone else."

And after going over these "terms & conditions" with GOD about my calling, I went on to add,

"And LORD JESUS, I've seen the reactions that people have toward the preacher. They can be standing talking on the corner, and when they see "Rev." they scatter like roaches after turning on the lights. LORD, let people be drawn to me. For what good is your message if no one is there to hear it".

And the many times I've told my testimony of how I got called to the Ministry, I know that the LORD accepted my terms, and proved it with the birth of a child, just like he said he would.

It's been 20 years come November; it's been rough but I've never looked back. And in spite of some rather heartbreaking times in my life, GOD has remained faithful. And the gifts that the LORD placed in the "Servant of GOD" Jesse Duplantis, has often helped me make it through the "darkness" in my life. No I never done drugs, drink, cuss like a sailor (pardon the term guys), or ran around with women. But if there was a party going on when I was growing up, the real fun & dancing didn't really start till "Finis" got there. So I can relate to Jesse to some degree, when it came to music & partying, hence the ministry name...

"JAMMIN4JESUS productions";

...But I don't play when it comes to the "things of GOD".

There are a few others that GOD used to lay the foundation for my teaching. "M.O.G." like Bishop T.D. Jakes, Dr. Lester Summeral, Joel Osteen's father, John Hagee, Joyce Meyers, Marilyn Hickey, Benny Hinn, Kenneth Copeland. All these people were strangers to me, when GOD first called me. I didn't know a "Copeland" from a "Dollar," but I soon learn. And each one had such an impact on my life that I wrote a Literary piece years ago called "Warriors for Christ". I carried a copy around for years in poster form; even gave one copy to Marilyn Hickey's ministry people during one of her visits here in New Orleans years ago. Don't know where a copy is now since I've moved so much over the years, and lost so much too. But maybe the copy I gave to Marilyn Hickey ministry might be stuck somewhere in a storage room behind some stuff; it would be a miracle if it still exist.

All these were men & women of GOD who helped shape my teaching & upbringing, and laying the foundation for how & what I was taught concerning Ministry. And along with my own pastor Eddie Holton that the Lord place me under, I received a pretty solid foundation when it came to biblical principles. And even back then GOD knew that regular Bible college wasn't gonna suit me, cause GOD knew I wasn't a regular kinda guy. HE also knew (without telling me) that HE wasn't gonna take me down a "regular road" to teach & preach this Gospel of Jesus Christ. Because if the LORD had shown me the "crazy roads" I would have to go down, and the "crazy things" I would suffer, I would have broke out running in the opposite direction. So HE never gives us a preview of where we would go; what we would suffer; and who would hurt & break our hearts. But HE is teaching us LOVE; HE is teaching us PATIENCE; HE is teaching us Scripture...and HE is teaching us by HIS HOLY SPIRIT. The ONE... who is here on earth with us; to lead & guide us into all TRUTH.

Well, having waited several weeks for the culmination of this highly anticipated conference, I was excited that the morning had finally arrived. I stayed at my sister's and slept on the floor so that I wouldn't have any trouble getting to City Church. I live on the West bank, and I wasn't taking any chances with missing this church service; it had been years since I saw Jesse in person.

I attended the Saturday night conference the night before, as well; leaving all my family members & their friends at the same sister's house that was right down from the church. We were celebrating the 12th birthday of her only grand-daughter (that would make here my great-niece) and of course there was enough food to feed a church. This was my sister's only grand-daughter, and since she really knows how to cook, she layed out quite a spread of food. Having had 5 boys of her own, and all grandsons until the granddaughter can along, you know this grandchild would be spoil rotten...but in a nice way. So there was quite a bit of food. But I had to leave; Pastor's Dad (Bishop McManus) was gonna be preaching, and it was indeed a special occasion. He talked about being "nailed in a sure place" during his message, and the message definitely applied to me in so many ways. This is what my life has been all about since being called to Ministry...

..."being where you suppose to be, when you suppose to be there; nailed in a sure place"...

...and, the essence and title of this 4 part book series, "12 months From Now".

The idea and concept for the book came to me when I first sat down on the pew at City Church almost 18 months ago. Yes, I recognize that at the moment, it's been way past 12 months since first put "pen to paper," at the leading of the Holy Spirit. But we would be fair in saying,

"There have been some unplanned & unexpected events that have delayed the books by a few months."

But it's all good.

I'm also working on a children's book for the holiday of October, as well as getting this book series out by the end of the year. It's a busy & difficult time for me (especially not having a place of my own yet), but that will change...and Soon...(in JESUS name)!.

I signed two contracts yesterday for a place, and I ASKED GOD for it (like Jesse said to do); I'm not trying to do it myself, so we will wait on GOD.

And at the end of Jesse's message at the 11'oclock service, Bishop did something that he said he never done before. So, WE are believing GOD for the miracles. I don't know how much I had in my wallet but I gave everything I had. It ain't much since I haven't gotten a normal wage in 2 years, but it was all I had. I had $40 dollars when I got to church, and made sure to get change from one of the ladies so I could put my $4.00 tithe in. But when Bishop spoke about his obeying GOD was a "supernatural offering" I wasn't gonna miss that...

...Mama ain't raised no fool!

I didn't fill in the amount cause I didn't check; I just gave everything I had in my wallet. Since coming back to church still unemployed in the conventional sense, I haven't been putting my name on my envelope. Admitting my partial embarrassment by the miniscule amount

I'm having to put in due to my not working right now, I didn't want no one thinking,

"Oh no he didn't!...SIR didn't put in no $2.00...what a cheapskate!"

A hundred dollars every Sunday was not unusual for me when I was working at my hospital jobs, or owning apartments. One Sunday I put in $400 dollars and I did it cheerfully because I know it was what I was lead to do.

So for the "supernatural" offering, I made sure to put my name though. I figure they could count and record the amount themselves. GOD knows my heart and knows what I have contributed to the kingdom. Plus, I don't allow people to put me in bondage when it comes to giving. But I made sure I put my name on the envelope so that the church have a record of my giving. So when the miracles start flowing, and they see my face in the crowd (and read this passage), they gonna know why,

"the money is chasing me (without me chasing it)".

During the service while Jesse was still preaching, I felt lead to go and buy the book that he mentioned he had for sell. He said it was a book he wrote years ago titled,

"The Everyday Visionary".

When I entered the foyer, I didn't see Keith his assistant. But as I was half way to the table where the items were covered pending sale, we nearly bumped into one another. I asked him if I could buy the book and he said,

"Sure, but it's the only copy I got".

So I knew right then and there that, that copy was brought in just for me. After buying the book from Keith...Steve Harvey's nephew...(you had to be there) for $16.00 dollars, I gave him one of the only $20 dollar bills I had left in my wallet after paying tithe from out of the other $20 dollar bill. I then told Keith,

"keep the change, and sow it to the ministry",

I hurried back to hear the rest of the message, as Jesse was about to close. But before I did, I gave Keith one of my business cards with my cell# written on the back. I just wanted to personally thank Jesse for all he'd done in my life personally, and I knew meeting him was out of the question. Ironically, I had met Jesse and shook his hand 20 years earlier, right in the breezeway in the rear between the two buildings I was standing in right then and there.. At the time the church was pastored by a different ministry and was called something else; Jesse Duplantis was invited there for a conference as well. It was my first time seeing him in person, and I was so excited that I wanted my then wife, and all my children to meet & see him in person. They all knew him from watching him on TV with me. My kids ages at the time were 11, 9, 7, 5, and 1; and they were as excited as I was to see this man that Daddy loved so much, and was so excited to see in person. After service was over, we headed to the back building to see if we could see him as he was leaving. When I saw him in the breezeway I yelled,

"Jesse!"

or maybe I said,

"Mr Duplantis"; I'm not sure which one

(its been so long ago). But he soon turned around an greeted me and my family, and shook my hand. That was a perfect ending to a great night with a great message to booth.

So I had my reasons for giving Keith one of my business cards to give Mr. Duplantis.

"I'm gonna put it right here in my shirt pocket to give to him" he said, as he place my infamous business card of me "dressed to the tee" with my "fly" hat on my head.

People see my business card and always say,

"Wow!...that's you SIR?"

Or, the youngsters would say,

"Dang, looka SIR!...Pimping for JESUS!

And I would just laugh to myself, and remember how the LORD gave me the idea for the Ministry's name, and the image for Ministry's business card. It seems to always leave an impression...and a good one at that.

Well, its been about 10 hours since I gave the card to Keith, but I ain't trippin. GOD's gonna hold him to his word. And if and when he does deliver the message, Jesse will then have a choice as well to "do something." But whatever comes of it, I just wanted to say,

"THANK YOU... JESSE DUPLANTIS!"

...for you and your wife, being obedient to the calling of GOD.

By the time I arrived back on the West

bank, I was pretty tired. I also learned today that Jesse was also an "Algiers boy" like myself. I always knew he was from New Orleans, but I never knew he was a fellow "Algierian" (Of course no one in their right mind would used that term to refer to ourselves)..ya might get shot (just kidding)...you would get a very strange look though.

"We are from the West bank...the Best Bank; and we ain't nuthin like those people from "across the river", is what you might hear.

And before Katrina, and before they started tearing down the "projects" you could tell the difference between the westbank & the eastbank people.. And since Hurricane Katrina we realize

"We are all in it together!"

One big city, with one big goal:

"Live...and make New Orleans a better place".

As I got back to the West bank, I just sat down and caught my breath. I wasn't even able to read my book that I bought. Since revamping my writing career, I've been reading books left & right. I think I've checked out about 20 in two weeks, and read about half, and glance thru the other half. I normally would go to my sister's after church and watch the Saints game with them. Since she is right in the neighborhood, I try to stop and spend time with my siblings. But my day started at 5am after waking up and not being able to go back to sleep. She asked me to come and join her at her church for 8am, to see their dance group dance; So that's where I was at

8am. Their dance routine was awesome; every time I visit with her church and witness their dance, I'm blown away. The music they've chosen to accompany their dance is usually incredibly anointed, and perfect for their routine. I cry every time because the anointing be so apparent. I know there are many people that sing & play gospel music, but all of it is not anointed. Since being around music all my life, and around all different types of genres, I know "Anointed" music, from music that just sounds good, or has a nice beat. And since Music speaks to the "Soul of man", I've learned that there are different levels and strengths of anointing within different types of music. And each type fulfills different needs. There is Anointing in music for healing; anointing for worship; anointing for praise; anointing for prayer; anointing for miracles; anointing for spiritual renewal.

And all the different types of music feeds different aspects of the "soul of man". The music either promotes the "light" in the world that is the "light & goodness of GOD," or the bad music promotes the "evil & darkness" in the world,. It is all self explanatory.

And just because it may be called "Gospel music", that don't make it automatically anointed.

Well, it is getting late; it's after 1a.m. I have a busy and important day tomorrow. I have to meet with an attorney about setting up some "Trust funds". I believe it's better to plan ahead when it comes to certain things, and since the plan is to be well-off and prosperous (and be a blessing to my children and other family members as well), I need to make preparations. Wealthy, healthy, & wise is the preparations that must be made.

I still have to get the children's book, "The GHOST in the Fourth Bedroom" to the printer in the next two days. My sister Cyn was suppose to do a proofread for me, but I haven't heard from her yet. I guess I'll call her tomorrow; she probably was too busy, but I'll check with her nevertheless. I know proof-reading your own material does nott work. You are reading it in your mind, and what's in your mind don't necessarily be what's on the paper.

So....,

"Buenos noches!"

"Hasta manana!"

...And LORD,

"speak to me in my dreams; show me visions when I'm awake,

and Holy Spirit, lead, guide, & teach me, so that I can teach others;

...in JESUS name, AMEN.

Saturday..... October 4, 2014... 8:11p.m.

Wow! Look at the time; I cannot believe I started to write this passage exactly 12 hours ago. I awaked at about 6:45am, but remained in the "prone position" till about 7:45 a.m. When I finally got up, I was thinking about money still (the lack there of), and wondered if GOD had came thru with something....anything. I had the $80 dollars from my unemployment, but was still short $20 to get the manuscript sent off. Then I remembered that I promised to send my daughter Diamond $40 dollars, and since I decided (long time ago) that their needs come before my own, I would be going to Wal-mart in a few minutes to send a Money gram. That would leave me short still, but oh well...such is life sometimes.

Then I began to think about the "supernatural offering" I put in the church last Sunday, and I thought of the "widow's mite. I guess you can call mine the "desperate divorcee (wallet empty/ain't got no mo)dollars." Either way, it was my last, and I was looking for a harvest.

Then another thought crossed my mind;

"What if nothing happens? What if no "supernatural miracle of a harvest" come thru?.

Then I started getting pissed,

"That was my last!...I went home with nothing in my pocket, nothing on my card, and nothing to buy food for 3 days!"

And when I checked the lottery ticket later on that I had laying around...

(yea I heard it all; Christians ain't suppose to gamble; I personally call it investing:.. I give you a dollar, you give me several million in return...not a bad investment by any standards)

...and saw it was worth just a dollar, I was even more pissed. Right then and there I started looking for Lab-top to make an entry for today, and spew out all my angry toward this "system of church offering & promises of financial miracles. I'd been down that road already, and I had no patience for going down there again.

Then I began thinking about why Pastors &

Preachers can say & preach what they preach about financial blessings. I looked around in my office and saw all the "Tim Coon's" books I owned, the Kenneth Copeland's on Financial blessings, LeSea, DayStar, T.D. Jakes, Marilyn Hickey, and Joel Osteen, to name a few...Of course they were blessed! They have complete strangers (Partners & members) sending them money every day, millions & millions of dollars, and I can't even raise a few bucks. They can't help but be...blessed! I remember not to long ago, I tried to get a few ministries to help me out with "preaching the Gospel". I sent out 10 letters asking for help; to 10 well known ministries, and 10 secular foundations. Only 1 from each, ever responded. Neither were able to help me, but I appreciated the kindness & caring they each exhibit by contacting me...and they both did so by phone. The others, never heard a word from them, or even received an email or postcard. So to say that I've lost a little respect for some, and not that impressed, would be correct.

Each day I learn that,

"Ever thing the glitters, ain't gold; and everyone that says LORD, LORD ain't talking bout Christ, or has the "people of GOD" best interest, at heart." It's a hard pill to swallow, but some are in it for the money and the "financial blessing." I read the tattoo on the arm of a young man to day. It said,

"Only GOD can judge me."

And I guess some think this statement is some kind of "get out of jail (hell)" card that they can use later, while they are living in Sin and disobeying the Word of GOD.

My response is simply,

"HE has judged you already.";

"...The scales have been weighed, and you are found wanting..."

Still thinking about the possibility that maybe I'd been duped again into believing I was gonna get this great financial blessing because I gave my last to the "supernatural offering' in church(like I've done so many times in the past), I was still a little mad. I grabbed my Lab-top expecting to make an entry, but I hit the wrong keys. I hit the saved key after trying to get the manuscript started, but when I opened the file again, something weird had happen. My paragraphs & pages that I'd already written were not lining up correctly. Frustrated by this obvious set-back, I saw no point in trying to continue to write. So now 13 hours later (it's now 9:36 p.m.), I'm finally making a comment on the subject. Maybe something was trying to keep me from talking about it, but if I'm mistaken about what I've said, GOD will let me know. And at that point I will apologize, and re-tract the statements made. If I'm correct in my observations, then I know some things are gonna change in the "Body of Christ."

I think I'll sleep now; I've written at least 4 hours straight today on two separate occasions. Once under a tree on the river (posted it on Facebook earlier), and now here in my office/ studio/ abode. Today was so cool, windy, and beautiful; without a doubt Fall (or Autumn as some would say) has definitely arrived. The nights are so much cooler; the days are windy (getting ready for Mr Winter's arrival); and the Sun is bright & sunny but not at all making the day hot & miserable. If I forgot to thank the LORD for such a beautiful day, I thank HIM now...

"LORD, thank you for such a wonderful & beautiful day today;

  it was one of those days, I saw your face...

basked in your grace...

let bad times all be erased...

and I was grateful having YOU in my space.

    We LOVE YOU Father GOD;.

    We LOVE YOU Holy Spirit;

    We LOVE YOU Jesus Christ...Amen.

Good nite my fellow Believers

(and Lovers of GOD)!

May the JOY of the LORD surrounds You,

And the Power of GOD forever astounds You,

And the Spirit of the LORD is always found within YOU;

Another day lies before US

, ...so don't give up,...or be afraid.

(I think I'll listen to "Love's Holiday" by Earth, Wind, & Fire)

SUNDAY...October 4, 2014; 5:27 pm

Well, the day has ended, and it has been a day that I did not plan. I knew that I didn't have any money, and not enough gas in my car, so the chance of getting to City Church was slim. But I told myself that I would just get up, and catch the bus. And if you live in New Orleans, and depend heavily on the Bus Service, you know there have been some days that you just didn't get where you were going on time. With it being the weekend as well, I knew I may not get there at all.

With the intent of going to both the 9am & 11am service, I knew I needed to get up by 6:30am. Unfortunately, it didn't work out that way; it was 9am by the time I awaken. The music for the first Service would have just started, so I decided to just focused on getting to the 11'oclock service instead.

I never made it to the 11'oclock Service, or to City Church for that matter. The Bus I had hoped to catch never arrived, and it was already 5 minutes to 10:00am. When I called the number posted on the sign to see what time the next bus would arrive, I had another hour wait. Somehow the bus I was running to try and beat to the bus stop, must have came a few minutes early...just my luck I thought. But then I said,

"LORD, maybe you have a different plan today?"

Looking over my shoulder, I knew there were two churches in the next block. One was a product of the Blake family ministry (which I had already visited once), and it was housed in the old "Abalon" theater. It was now a church called "New Home," and I can remember when I last saw Bishop Blake Sr. and his lovely wife preach there years ago. The name of the current Pastor escapes me, but I had visited with them a few months earlier when I was still friends with one of its members. We aren't friends any longer, and I think it's a typical occurrence with some so-called Christians.

A simple misunderstanding was taken personally and blown out of proportion; made even worse by a later incident. So going to "New Home" was out of the question.

The other church was also housed in an old theater, and this is where I felt I was being lead to go. I don't know why, but I've learn to just follow orders (the leading of the Holy Spirit).

I had attended this church as well, many years ago; but not since they had moved to this new location. The Pastor & his wife I knew both growing up, but not personally. The wife, who was now Prophetess Casimere I remember from us both attending Edna Karr Jr. High. The first time I heard & saw her preach, the anointing on her, was as visible as her caramel brown skin. There was no denying that GOD's hand was indeed upon her Life.

So with no plans of my own, I found myself walking into LOVE OUTREACH CHRISTIAN CHURCH (LOCC), not having a clue of what was in store. I knew one thing though, if GOD sent me there, there was a reason; I was sent with a purpose; and GOD was ready to do something.

Later pondering the day, it dawn on me that when I started this 4-part Book series, I thought that I was just on a mission to find a Church home. Then I began to look back on where he has sent me in the past.

I began to realize that something much bigger was going on;....much, much bigger.

I've sat in Mega Churches; I've sat in small churches. Sometimes if I find myself walking or riding and it's a Wednesday, I might sneak in and sat in on a Bible study. In the back inconspicuous, waiting to see what the LORD want to show and/or teach me. I always make it a point to put something in the offering (even if all I have is "change" in my pocket), and always honor the "man of GOD" by shaking his hand and introducing myself before I leave. I'm always amazed at some of the things that GOD shows me.

One time before I started attending the Potter's house in Dallas, I was lead to attend a little church in Forth Worth called "New Beginnings." It was quite an appropriate name because my wife and I was in the midst of a "new beginning" ourselves. It wasn't until about two or three visit, that I realized why I was there. The Pastor was having kidney problems, and I saw satan literally trying to kill him. I believe he was on dialysis at that point, and his "flock" was literally doing nothing.

One service (not sure if it was Bible study or Sunday) I boldly stood up and told the people of GOD what "thus saith the LORD"...

"Why are ya'll just standing by and watching the enemy try and take out your Pastor! You all need to cover him; Pray for him, and keep praying for him. Don't you know he has an assignment, and the enemy is trying to TAKE HIS LIFE!"

From then on they began to "cover" the "man of GOD", and he began to do much better.

I continue to go a few more services, but when GOD gave me my release, I prepared to move on. Before leaving, I sat down with the Pastor (Pastor Don), and told him that I would be moving on. And I remember him asking me to stay a while longer until I find a church. I told him I couldn't; I had made that mistake once before, and I wasn't about to go down that road again.

Pastor had gotten comfortable with seeing me there; but he said something to me once that reflected quite the opposite. We were having a one on one conversation, and I don't quite remember the context of the conversation, but I know it was about the church, and some of the things that I saw were going on in the church. And I remember him clearly telling me...

"You speak pretty boldly, and some people (members) are offended by what you say."

I later thought about it and I realized that the only person that was offended was him. I came in; spoke with authority (given unto me by GOD); and set some order in the "House of GOD". Because GOD showed me that the devil was out to kill the "head". And the "sheep" was not aware of it, and was endanger of being scattered and become a victim of satan's many devices as well. So I guess some very bold words were spoken. But GOD never call me to make friends; HE called me to first:

1. Live the Gospel;

2. then preach & teach it as HE turn the hearts of "men" to CHRIST;..and the former "children of GOD", ...BACK to CHRIST.

3. To teach the young people that Life is not all fun and games; there is a real devil; and he don't discriminate. He kills REAL children. And if they are in the dark, and don't have the knowledge, and a

relationship with CHRIST,...they will become a victim too.

4. Teach the older generation; these are not the "days of old"; we are living in a "new day" and we are being given "new wine". So that GOD can do a "new thing."

5. To heal the sick (no matter what form it has manifested); cast out the demons; and come against the kingdom of darkness, and the workers of Sin & Evil.

6. Point at the "systems of corruptions...call them out...PRAY...and "tear them down".

7. And lastly, let the world know "every knee shall bow, and every tongue shall confess that...JESUS IS LORD!...and no man come into the Father except thru the SON (which is CHRIST JESUS). So whatever religion you are a part of that says contrary...tell the world, it's all LIES!

This is the mandate that the LORD has given me concerning the "Kingdom of GOD" and the office & authority he has placed under my stewardship.

For the Ushering in, and the "2nd Coming of Jesus Christ" will soon be upon Us. And if the "Body of Christ" is not making preparations, and is in the dark, then we have failed in our duties of Preaching, Teaching, and revealing the mysteries of GOD, and the Gospel of JESUS CHRIST!

Service was interesting; as I walked in, it was great to see the "people of GOD" worshipping in Music to usher in the presence of GOD. I don't see that to often. People usually just come into the sanctuary like it's just another place. But it is "suppose to be" the HOUSE OF THE LORD.

And one should come into the presence of GOD, humble, with thanksgiving, and with praise...so seeing this "blessed my soul" . During a few of the songs, the tears just flowed, because I know where GOD had brought me from, and what HE had brought me through.

Then later on, someone (a young woman) walked up to the front and began to pray. It wasn't long before, I had to pray as well. As she was praying...

"oh Lord, forgive us of our sins... we need to repent Lord... oh we are a sinful nation...we have not kept your word..."

I detected a "condemnation spirit" and I began to pray against that thing. We are the "righteous of Christ Jesus," and if she needed to repent of something then she needed to repent, but began to pray a "spirit of praise" to come into the House...

"Oh Lord we thank You, we Praise You, and we Lift you up because You are GOD...We give you honor & praise...we sing holy, holy, to thy name.. blesseth is the Lord God...for we are the righteousness of Christ Jesus..."

And as I prayed, I saw the atmosphere shift back, and the "spirit of praise" returned. She probably didn't realize what she was doing, and I'm sure she meant well, but good intentions don't amount to a hill of beans. I learned a principal years ago from a fellow servant, and he said,

" The road to Hell, is paved with a lot of "good intentions."

So knowing what I now know, I'm not gonna just stand by, and watch people perish. You say or do something contrary to the Word and Will of GOD, I'm gonna pray against it...cause I know better. And I'm required to do, and be better.

I didn't know it was first Communion (are first Sunday for that matter), so of course I was excited about that. I don't remember the last time I took Communion, and I don't know how I've never taken it at City Church. If I did, I'm sure it was only once.

During the walk up to take Communion, I made it a point to shake the Pastor's hand and say,

"I'd like to speak with you after service."

I wasn't sure of all I would ask Pastor, but the first thing I was going to ask was,

"What is the Vision GOD has given you for this church, and what role are you to play in this community?"

When it was all said and done, we must have talked standing out in front the church, for an hour & a half, or more. I even got to look at some property (vacant land) that the church own. I told him as he was dropping me off afterwards, and I was exiting his car I said,

"I don't know why GOD sent me, but if He sent me here (LOVE OUTREACH CHRISTIAN CHURCH), even if it is for a season, this I know;

HE is about to do something in this House,

.and you better (need to) get ready!"

T H E E N D

...of Book III

This is where I've been lead to stop, and end BOOK III. July of 2013 is when Book I began; it is now October 2014, and almost 15 months have passed. A lot has happened, and a lot has been learn. As for Book IV; let's wait awhile...it may get even more interesting.

(pause)

(pain in my stomach; must have been the dinner I got from church ...pasta & chicken...because that's all I've eaten today; it was delicious though; and I KNOW I blessed my food before I ate...the pain has passed)

As I was saying...Book II is missing quite a few entries because it was during some of my "rough times" and I had no transportation. Looking back, I could have caught a ride with my old schoolmate's son (the one GOD used to get me going to City Church) but I'm still having trouble being on the receiving end of kindness...I'm getting better though. The time I had internet access, I may have watch one or two services, but overall I missed a lot.

I can't lose sleep over it though; I do what I can, and if I can't get something done I just go to GOD and ask,

"Where did I go wrong?"

The hardest part of the previous 15 months though have been the times I've been without my 3 daughters. The eldest will be making 7 in 12 days(one day after her mother make a birthday, and the middle child will be 6 the following month (4 days before my birthday). And it was the birthday of the youngest (she made 4) when the mother came last year, and stole all 3 of them. So it's been 7 months since I've seen them, and only once since I spoke with them on the phone. Several weeks ago she had the audacity to call and ask me for money; I laughed.

She should have thought of the outcome of her actions before she did what she did, Lied and had me thrown in jail, and now let the govt prostitute her with government assistance while she bring bastards in the world conceived with whoremongers.

...a little harsh?

Well it was even worse when I had to live through it.

It has indeed been a rough road; I learned a lot, all has been forgiven, and the plan of GOD didn't change. The mantel was still on my LIFE to Live, Preach, and Teach the Gospel of Jesus Christ. And notice I always say the "Gospel of Jesus Christ" because I've learned that there are all kinds of "gospels" out their being preach. And I dare not join that group. If the message that is coming out of your mouth (as you preach the Gospel) is not perpetuating, promoting, or saturated with the "Spirit of LOVE"...it ain't CHRIST, and it ain't HIS Gospel.

I'm SIR...the "SOUL"man; and I know what you read a moment ago sounded pretty harsh. But you know, the Truth is sometimes harsh, and sometimes hurts. And to live some of the things that I had to live hurt me very, very much. But when I got married the 2nd time, GOD spoke to me about that wife and said,

"Read the "Book of Hosea."

And if you know anything about the book, you know it speaks loud & clear about one thing...forgiveness. I had to learn this, and I learned it the hard way...but I learned it. And I'm better for it, and I would not be the "man of GOD" that I AM if it was not for...

LOVE;

for JOY;

for FORGIVENESS:

for PATIENCE;

and for the CHRIST that lives within me. And if we all can get there, we'll see GOD, and spent eternity in Heaven.

But...If we never learn to...LOVE, and FORGIVE

(You can't do one without the other),

WE WILL NEVER SEE GOD, or see HEAVEN.

Now if this "past life" concept is true,

(like I touched on earlier; I think the concept requires more looking into...praying & fasting... cause it doesn't all add up to me, but it's interesting)

then we'll just keep coming back until we get it...

...Learn how **to LOVE,**

& FORGIVE.

<u>Last word (for the married ones):</u>

With all that I've experienced in this area of life, this is what I have learned. When we have a spouse that GOD has placed in our lives, in spite of what the world says & teaches, GOD wants U.S. to forgive & stay together. That's what GOD wants; no matter what they have done, ...YOU HAVE NO CASE AGAINST THEM. That's what Calvary was for; so Forgive,

Forget,

And stay together.

(Now if GOD didn't put you both together...that's a different story;... END IT!)

BE BLESS, People & Children of GOD!

...JESUS is Coming Back SOON!

(Sooner than you think)

.

...The end (again)

www.ingramcontent.com/pod-product-compliance
Lightning Source LLC
Chambersburg PA
CBHW061451040426
42450CB00007B/1306